HUMAN IMPACT ON EARTH: CAUSE AND EFFECT

CHANGING PLAINS ENVIRONMENTS

LISA IDZIKOWSKI

PowerKiDS press

New York

Published in 2020 by The Rosen Publishing Group, Inc.
29 East 21st Street, New York, NY 10010

First Edition

Editor: Jane Katirgis
Book Design: Reann Nye

Photo Credits: Series art Xiebiyun/Shutterstock.com; Alexander Tolstykh/Shutterstock.com; Cafe Racer/Shutterstock.com; cover Thomas Welborn/Moment Open/Getty Images; p. 5 David Fossler/Shutterstock.com; p. 7 kungfoofoto/Shutterstock.com; p. 8 Sergey Nesterchuk/Shutterstock.com; p. 9 James Gabbert/Shutterstock.com; p. 10 Sasha Samardzija/Shutterstock.com; p. 11 Kevin Russ/Moment/Getty Images; p. 12 Buyenlarge/Archive Photos/Getty Images; p. 13 Ghost Bear/Shutterstock.com; p. 15 Kerry Hargrove/Shutterstock.com; p. 16 Pictureguy/Shutterstock.com; p. 17 Courtesy of the Library of Congress; p. 19 PhotoQuest/Archive Photos/Getty Images; p. 20 MPI/Archive Photos/Getty Images; p. 21 Everett Historical/Shutterstock.com; p. 23 KARI K/Shutterstock.com; p. 24 Tim Zurowski/Shutterstock.com; p. 25 Arina P Habich/Shutterstock.com; p. 26 Thomas Bresenhuber/Shutterstock.com; p. 27 Dmitriy Kandinskiy/Shutterstock.com; p. 28 aslysun/Shutterstock.com; p. 29 Ashley Whitworth/Shutterstock.com; p. 30 iko/Shutterstock.com.

Cataloging-in-Publication Data

Names: Idzikowski, Lisa.
Title: Changing plains environments / Lisa Idzikowski.
Description: New York : PowerKids Press, 2020. | Series: Human impact on Earth: cause and effect | Includes glossary and index.
Identifiers: ISBN 9781725301320 (pbk.) | ISBN 9781725301344 (library bound) | ISBN 9781725301337 (6pack)
Subjects: LCSH: Plains-Juvenile literature.
Classification: LCC GB572.I36 2020 | DDC 551.45'3-dc23

Manufactured in the United States of America

CPSIA Compliance Information: Batch #CSPK19. For Further Information contact Rosen Publishing, New York, New York at 1-800-237-9932.

CONTENTS

PLAINS ENVIRONMENTS

Plains are one type of landform on Earth's surface. They cover about one-third of the land. Wide and mostly flat, plains appear on every continent. Not all look the same, however. Some are quite large, and the plants and animals found on individual plains can be very different. It just depends on the climate and the geography of each location.

Before human history, plants and animals thrived in plains around the world. When people arrived and settled these natural areas, they made a big impact, often negative. Animals were hunted for food—some to **extinction**. In modern times, plains were destroyed by plowing and fencing. This ruined **native** habitats, and in certain areas problems developed, such as the Dust Bowl in North America.

IMPACT FACTS

Earth isn't the only planet where plains are found. Mercury and Mars have plains too!

Some plains are so vast that the land and sky seem to stretch on without end.

HOW DO PLAINS FORM?

Plains generally are located toward the center of continents or along the shore of oceans and rivers. The Great Plains of North America lies in the center of the United States. The Serengeti stretches through central Africa, and the West Siberian Plain covers central Russia. The Atlantic Coastal Plain forms the eastern shore of the United States. The Nile River **floodplain** follows the path of the Nile River in Egypt.

Natural forces create three main types of plains. Erosional plains form when land is smoothed over and flattened by wind, water, or glaciers. Depositional plains develop as materials such as rocks and soil are scattered over an area by wind, water, or even lava. And structural plains developed when Earth first formed.

IMPACT FACTS

Around the world, grasslands have different names: North America has prairies, South America has pampas, Africa has savannas, and Eurasia has **steppes**.

Plains are wide, flat landforms. They're perfect for grazing cattle. They're also a great place to visit to admire the beauty of nature.

LANDS OF GRASS

Rhodes grass, red oat grass, blue grama, buffalo grass, and blazing stars. Grasses and some flowers make up the common vegetation of many plains. Depending on weather and geography, grasslands can be classified into two main groups. Savannas flourish under warm conditions. They cover almost half of Africa and large parts of Australia, India, and South America. Temperate grasslands need areas with hot summers and cold winters. These grasslands spread across Russia, Hungary, Argentina, Canada, and the United States.

NORTH AMERICA'S GREAT PLAINS

The Great Plains covers a vast area of land. About one-fourth of the North American continent is a part of these plains. The area runs from Canada in the north to Texas in the south. It spans west beyond the forests of the Midwest all the way to the Rocky Mountains. It is a place of almost endless sky that seems to stretch on forever.

Parts of ten states make up most of the Great Plains: Colorado, Kansas, Montana, Nebraska, New Mexico, North Dakota, Oklahoma, South Dakota, Texas, and Wyoming.

STRETCHING INTO CANADA

The Great Plains extends northward into the provinces of Canada. Parts of Manitoba, Alberta, Saskatchewan, and the Northwest Territories join with the ten states in the United States to make up the area. The total area of the Great Plains is about 1,125,000 square miles (2,900,000 square km).

On the Great Plains, the weather changes by the season and location. Summers are usually wet. Winters are drier. The eastern parts commonly receive more precipitation than the west. And the temperature changes from north to south. Generally, it gets warmer going farther south. At one time, this area was called the Great American Desert.

THE EARLY GREAT PLAINS ENVIRONMENT

A very active environment shaped the Great Plains during the Pleistocene era. This period in Earth's history began about 2.6 million years ago and was marked by changing weather patterns. During this time, cycles of massive glaciers formed the Great Plains.

Paleontologists have unearthed fossil bones of the animal life from this time. The Great Plains supported giant-sized mammals including mammoths, mastodons, saber-toothed cats, ground sloths, camels, bears, wolves, and others. These giants vanished near the end of the Pleistocene era, around 11,000 to 12,000 years ago.

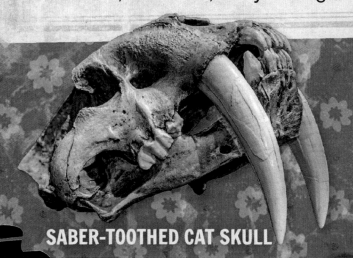

SABER-TOOTHED CAT SKULL

WHAT HAPPENED TO THE GIANTS?

Dr. Ross MacPhee of the American Museum of Natural History in New York believes that three possible causes might be to blame for the extinction of very large mammals, such as mastadons. One idea, "overkill," puts human hunters squarely to blame. Another idea, "overchill," says that climate changes were the reason. And the third belief is that some space object hit Earth, setting the "overgrill" in motion.

Bison played an important part in the Great Plains grassland **ecosystem**.

In more recent times, another set of animals had settled the area. Early explorers saw pronghorns, coyotes, and grizzly bears. Bison, which survived the earlier extinction, roamed the plains in great herds.

NATIVE AMERICANS AND THE GREAT PLAINS

Native Americans lived on the Great Plains and supported themselves in different ways. Many tribes hunted for bison, antelope, deer, elk, small animals, birds, and fish. They grew corn, squash, sunflowers, and beans. They also gathered wild plants, such as berries, that served as food and medicine. Bison played a huge part in the life of Plains society. Besides food, the powerful animals provided fur and skins for clothing and shelter, and horns and bones for tools.

IMPACT FACTS

Plains Indians intentionally burned large areas of grasslands to make it easier to hunt the huge herds of bison.

North American horses became extinct between 8,000 and 12,000 years ago. The horses in North America today are relatives of horses Spanish explorers brought with them starting in the 1400s.

Some Plains tribes lived in established settlements while others favored an active life, moving from place to place as they hunted. Hunters went after their prey animals on foot until later when they obtained horses. Plains Indians adopted a style of life fitted to their environment. They respected nature and the environment.

13

PIONEER SETTLEMENT OF THE PLAINS

Starting in the early 19th century, pioneer settlers flowed in from many different areas and swamped the Great Plains. Lucky travelers riding stagecoaches westward witnessed herds of bison and pronghorn spread across the grassland almost as far as they could see to the horizon. Black-footed ferrets, prairie dogs, prairie chickens, badgers, rattlesnakes, grasshoppers, and other animals shared this environment.

Unfortunately, European settlers did not respect the Plains ecosystem and its wondrous wildlife. Unlike Native Americans, they did not use the natural resources wisely. They viewed this great mass of wildlife as something to be taken, often for pure sport. Hunters killed almost everything that stomped, soared, scampered, and skittered across the landscape. John James Audubon, a famous **naturalist**, once said that "Surely, this should not be permitted."

IMPACT FACTS

It is estimated that the population of bison once numbered around 30 to 50 million animals. By the 1890s, fewer than 1,000 animals survived.

Black-footed ferrets once filled the prairies of the Great Plains. But there are now only about 300 of this highly endangered animal.

FARMING THE GREAT PLAINS

Early settlers brought their farming practices with them as they moved onto the Plains. Many came from the eastern states where they grew corn and wheat and raised cattle. Naturally, they wanted to continue this type of farming. A surprise waited for them in the West—prairie grasslands of thick, heavy sod. Back-breaking work was needed before the land could be farmed. John Lane invented a special type of plow in 1833. This plow may have conquered the sod but not the difficult weather conditions.

IMPACT FACTS

By the mid 1850s, the John Deere factory had improved the original plow design of John Lane and was selling more than 10,000 plows each year.

Newly arrived farmers depended on the plow to break up tough prairie sod.

In the summer, it could be blazing hot. Then winters turned bitterly cold. Successful crops needed water, too. Some years enough rainfall kept crops growing, but during other years it was like a desert. Difficult conditions didn't stop the settlers. The natural prairie kept disappearing under the plow.

17

DUST BOWL YEARS

Who could imagine a solid wall of wind and dirt? Wheat that didn't grow? Animals that couldn't breathe? In the early 20th century, people seeking land streamed west. Many were from Europe or areas in the United States where cheap land was no longer available. Again, the grasslands of the Great Plains lost out to the plow. But this time it was a gas-powered machine that dug at the sod day and night.

Thousands of acres of wheat **displaced** natural buffalo grass. Some years there was enough rain—until there wasn't, and a **drought** began. Crops dried up and died. Soil lay bare. Winds howled and whipped up great walls of dirt and sand that swept over the Plains. America's Dust Bowl, a human-made environmental disaster, took over.

"Black blizzards" hit the Plains during the Dust Bowl. These dust storms darkened the sky and could last for several days.

WHO'S TO BLAME?

The United States government was partly to blame for the Dust Bowl. Three government acts fired up a mass of inexperienced farmers to invade the Great Plains. With so many people trying to make money farming, they plowed up more and more of the natural grasslands. The prairie grass that was perfectly suited to this environment was gone. And with it went the protective plants that kept soil from blowing away in the constant, strong winds.

HOW DID THE DUST BOWL END?

It was one of the most terrible storms in U.S. history. "Black Sunday," the worst storm of the Dust Bowl, occurred on April 14, 1935. Experts estimate that 3 million tons of topsoil took to the air on this day in the Great Plains. People caught in the storm must have wondered if it would ever end.

As members of the Civilian Conservation Corp, people helped plant trees.

Franklin D. Roosevelt was president at this time. He knew he had to act fast: help the people, help the environment, and stop the Dust Bowl. With the aid of Congress, the Soil Erosion Service and the Prairie States Forestry Project were put into place. These two agencies began **restoring** the damaged Plains ecosystem by encouraging new farming methods and a system of planting trees as windbreaks.

21

Populations keep edging up. People need food, energy, and shelter. Where is much of this food grown today? The Great Plains supplies a large amount, with wheat, corn, soy, and canola being key crops. Of course, there is good news and bad news about this. According to the World Wildlife Fund (WWF), about one-half of the entire Great Plains remains unharmed. But about 1.7 million acres (700,000 ha) was lost when it was plowed for farming in 2017. More grassland is also being used for increased energy and housing needs. And plowing up the prairie also harms drinking water.

But some Plains farmers have gotten smart! They are replanting the prairies. They are using fewer harmful chemicals and improving the soil. And most importantly, they are convincing others to adopt these new ways.

IMPACT FACTS

The World Wildlife Fund has a dedicated goal for 2030. It aims to stop the destruction of grasslands in the Northern Great Plains by that year.

PRAIRIE
RESTORATION
IN
PROG•RESS

In some areas, prairies are
actively being restored.

A GREAT IDEA!

At one time, ranchers and environmentalists might have been facing off and fighting one another. Now, however, many people are working together to restore prairie ecosystems. In Montana, ranchers and biologists are teaming up.

According to some scientists, Great Plains grassland songbirds have gone down in numbers by about 70 percent since 1970. What's the reason? Older farming practices, the need for more and more crops and housing, and climate change are to blame.

A chestnut-collared longspur is one bird of the Great Plains that is being threatened by the loss of native grasslands.

IMPACT FACTS

The Northern Great Plains Joint Venture (NGPJV) works to protect and restore native habitats for birds.

It's a good thing some ranchers are pulling up their cowboy boots and jumping into action. What are they doing exactly? They are using fewer chemicals on their land. They are choosing where cattle roam. And they are letting the native grasses come back. These efforts help wildlife, but they also provide people with cleaner water resources.

OTHER PLAINS AROUND THE WORLD

The Serengeti—or "endless plains" in the **Maasai** language—is a large plain in east-central Africa. A huge part is protected as a national park with grasslands and woodlands. The Serengeti's biggest attraction is its importance for animal **migration**. Over 1.5 million animals make a yearly round trip across the Serengeti. The biggest challenges facing the Serengeti include illegal hunting and habitat destruction.

ANCIENT GRASSLAND RESTORATION

Since the late 1980s, scientists in Russia have been trying to bring back an ancient grassland ecosystem. This steppe environment disappeared about 12,000 years ago, and with it, its stock of Pleistocene **herbivores**. The goal of "Pleistocene Park" and its new grazing animals is to restore the grasslands. If it works, the Siberian permafrost will stay intact and greatly aid efforts to stall climate change.

Evergreen trees with needles—such as pines, spruces, hemlocks, and firs—fill Siberian forests. Here the average temperature can be below freezing for six months of the year.

Another of the world's largest plains is in central Russia. Because of its immense size, the West Siberian Plain covers tundra, forest, and steppe or grassland ecosystems. Huge reserves of oil, natural gas, and minerals are proving both good and bad. Native reindeer herders are losing out to oil companies. One tribe, the Khanty, are fighting for their lands. They insist they cannot live without the forest, reindeer, snow, and white light.

The Salisbury Plain is a mostly treeless plain in England. Interestingly, underneath the surface is a form of limestone known as chalk. In prehistoric times, this area was heavily populated. These early people left behind remains of their culture in the form of stone monuments. Stonehenge is the most well-known. In addition to its ancient stone circles, the area is a designated Special Area of Conservation with rare plants and animals.

The ancient stone circle at Stonehenge is a monument to its prehistoric builders.

Grasslands and grassy woodlands once covered Australia's Cumberland Plain in western Sydney. But as with other plains around the world, this area was cleared for farming and settlement. Major conservation efforts have been underway for a number of years to replace weeds with native plant species and to restore more natural bushland.

29

CHALLENGING BUT HOPEFUL

Plains environments around the world have changed for millions of years. Some changes came as a result of Earth's natural forces. Wind, water, glaciers, and even volcanoes changed plains landforms. But this was part of nature, not manufactured or human-made. Human beings also played a major role in the transformation of natural systems. Plains were dug up and destroyed. Animals were hunted—sometimes until they disappeared. Crops took the place of native grasses. And fences interrupted the almost endless spaces.

Fortunately, people took notice. Countries realized they had to protect endangered plants and animals like bison and elephants. They created national parks and conservation areas. Hopefully, these efforts will continue as governments, scientists, and citizens around the world work to save and restore nature's native plains environments.

GLOSSARY

displaced: Something that has been replaced.

drought: A long period of time with little or no rain.

ecosystem: A group of living and non-living things in a certain environment.

extinction: When a plant or animal species dies out completely with none left alive.

floodplain: Land that is built up from soil that has overflowed a river.

herbivore: An animal that eats only plants.

Maasai: Members of pasturing and hunting people in Africa (Kenya and Tanzania).

migration: Moving from one place to another on a regular basis.

native: Living or growing naturally in a particular area.

naturalist: A person studying plants and animals in nature.

paleontologist: A scientist who studies animal and plant fossils.

restore: To return something to an original condition.

steppe: The term for grasslands found in Asia and southeastern Europe.

WEBSITES

Due to the changing nature of Internet links, PowerKids Press has developed an online list of websites related to the subject of this book. This site is updated regularly. Please use this link to access the list: www.powerkidslinks.com/HIOE/plains